*ANALYSIS AND ASSESSMENT*
*OF GATEWAY PROCESS*

# CIA

# ANALYSIS AND ASSESSMENT OF GATEWAY PROCESS

*(1983)*

*BY*

# WAYNE M. MCDONNELL

DEPARTMENT OF THE ARMY

US ARMY OPERATIONAL GROUP
US ARMY INTELLIGENCE AND SECURITY COMMAND
FORT GEORGE G. MEADE, MARYLAND 20755

*ISBN: 978-1-963956-03-0*

# Contents

IAGPC-O
9 June 1983
SUBJECT: Analysis and Assessment of Gateway Process

TO:Commander
US Army Operational Group
Fort Meade, MD 20755

1. You tasked me to provide an assessment of the Gateway Experience in terms of its mechanics and ultimate practicality. As I set out to fulfill that tasking it soon became clear that in order to assess the validity and practicality of the process I needed to do enough supporting research and analysis to fully understand how and why the process works. Frankly, sir, that proved to be an extremely involved and difficult business. Initially, based on conversations with a physician who took the Gateway training with me, I had recourse to the biomedical models developed by Itzhak Bentov to obtain information concerning the physical aspects of the process. Then I found it necessary to delve into various sources for information concerning quantum mechanics in order to be able to describe the nature and functioning of human consciousness. I had to be able to construct a scientifically valid and reasonably lucid model of the time-space dimension and the means by which expanded human consciousness transcends it in achieving Gateway's objectives. Finally, I again found it necessary to use physics to bring the whole phenomenon of out-of-body states into the language of physical science to remove the stigma of its occult connotations, and put it in a frame of reference suited to objective assessment.

2. I began the narrative by briefly profiling the fundamental biomedical factors affecting such related techniques as hypnosis, biofeedback and transcendental meditation so that their objectives and mode of functioning could be compared in the reader's mind with the Gateway experience as the model of its underlying mechanics was developed. Additionally, that introductory material is useful in supporting the conclusions of the paper. I indicate that at times these related techniques may provide useful entry points to accelerate movement into the Gateway Experience.

3. Niels Bohr, the renowned physicist once responded to his son's complaints about the obtuse nature of certain concepts in physics by saying: "You are not thinking, you are merely being logical." The physics of altered human consciousness deals with some conceptualizations that are not easily grasped or visualized exclusively in the context of ordinary "left brain" linear thinking. So, to borrow Dr. Bohr's mode of expression,

parts of this paper will require not only logic but a touch of right brain intuitive insight to achieve a complete comfortable grasp of the concepts involved. Nevertheless, once that is done, I am confident that their construction and application will stand up to the test of rational critique.

4. Paradoxically, having gone to such great lengths to avoid trying to render judgements based on an occult or dogmatic frame of reference in the end I found it necessary to return, at least briefly, to the question of the impact of the Gateway Experience on common belief systems. I did so because although it was essential to avoid attempting to render an assessment in the context of such systems, I felt that it was necessary after having completed the analysis to point out that the resulting conclusions do not have any violence to the fundamental mainstream of either eastern or western belief systems. Unless that point is clearly established, the danger exists that some people will reject the whole concept of the Gateway Experience in the mistaken belief that it contradicts and is therefore alien to all that they hold to be right and true.

5. This study is certainly not designed to be the last word on the subject but I hope that the validity of its basic structure and of the fundamental concepts upon which it is based will make it a useful guide for other USAINSCOM personnel who are required to take the Gateway training or work with Gateway materials.

WAYNE M. MCDONNELL
LTC, MI
Commander, Det O

The Gateway Experience: Brain Hemisphere Synchronization in perspective.

# 1. Introduction.

In order to describe the Monroe Institute technique for achieving altered states of consciousness(the "Gateway Experience") involving brain hemisphere synchronization or "Hemi-Sync", the most effective way to begin is to briefly profile the basic mechanics which underlay operation of related methods such as hypnosis, transcendental meditation, and biofeedback. It is easiest to effectively describe what Gateway is by beginning with a short description of those associated techniques that share some common aspects with the Gateway Experience but which are nevertheless different. In this way we can develop a frame of reference at the outset which will provide useful concepts to explain and understand Gateway by comparison, as we proceed.

## 2. Hypnosis.

According to the theories of psychologist Ronald Stone and the biomedical engineering models of Itshak Bentov, hypnosis is basically a technique which permits acquisition of direct access to the sensory motor cortex and pleasure centers, and lower cerebral(emotional) portions(and associated pleasure centers) of the right side of the human brain following successful disengagement of the stimulus screening function of the left hemisphere of the brain. The left hemisphere of the brain is the self-cognitive, verbal and linear reasoning component of the mind. It fulfills the function of screening incoming stimuli by categorizing, assessing and assigning meaning prior to allowing passage to the right hemisphere of the mind. The right hemisphere, which functions as the noncritical, holistic, nonverbal and pattern-oriented component of the brain appears to accept what the left hemisphere passes to it without question. Consequently, if the left hemisphere can be distracted either through boredom or through reduction to a soporific, semi-sleep state, external stimuli to include hypnotic suggestions are allowed to pass unchallenged into the right hemisphere where they are accepted and acted upon directly.

The result may involve an emotional reaction originating in the lower cerebral region, sensory/motor responses requiring involvement of the cortex, and so on. Both the sensory and the motor cortices of the right cerebral portion of the brain contain a sequence of points known as the "homunculus" which corresponds to points in the body(see Exhibit 1, next page). Stimulation of the corresponding area on the cortex causes intermediate response in the associated portion of the body. Consequently, induction of the suggestion that the left leg is numb, if it reaches the right hemisphere unchallenged and is referred to the appropriate area of the sensory cortex, will result in an electrical reaction being generated that will induce the feeling of numbness, Similarly, the suggestion that the person is experiencing a general feeling of happiness and well being would be referred to the appropriate pleasure centers located in the lower cerebral portion or in the cortex of the right hemisphere, thereby inducing the suggested feeling of euphoria. Finally, suggestions such as one that informs the hypnotic subject that he enjoys enhanced concentration or powers of memory would be responded to in the right hemisphere by accessing unused information storage capacity normally held in reserve as a result of left hemisphere selection and control processes. This aspect will become significant in the context of the Gateway process when attention is given to examining the way that hypnosis may be used to accelerate progress in the early stages of the Gateway Experience.

## 3. Transcendental Meditation.

On the other hand, transcendental meditation works in a distinctly different fashion. In this technique, intense and protracted single minded concentration on the process of drawing energy up the spinal cord ultimately results in what appears to be creation of acoustical standing waves in the cerebral ventricles which are then conducted to the gray matter in the cerebral

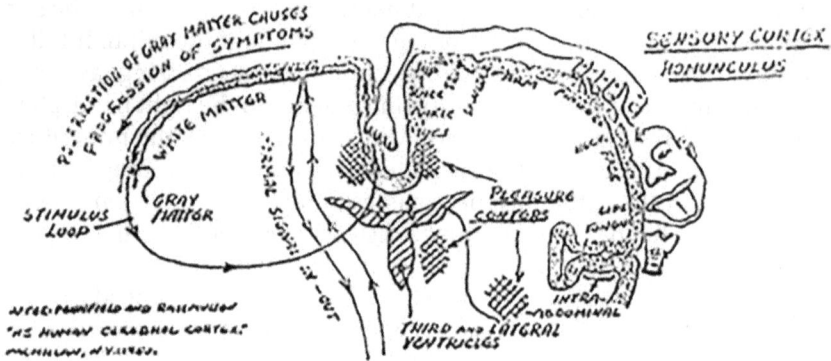

Figure A  The Homunculus

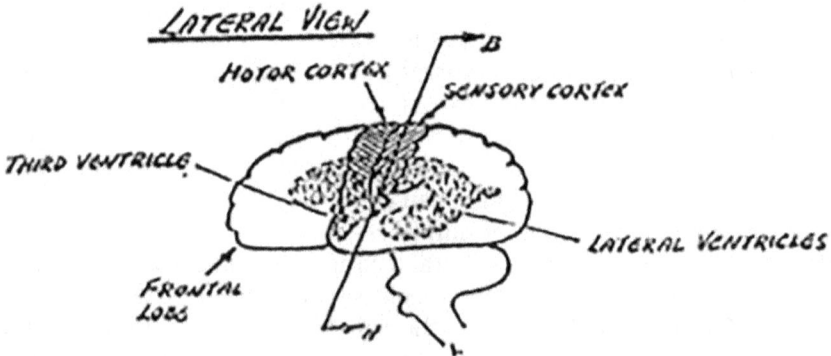

Figure B The Motor and Sensory Cortex and the Third and Lateral Ventricles

EXHIBIT 1

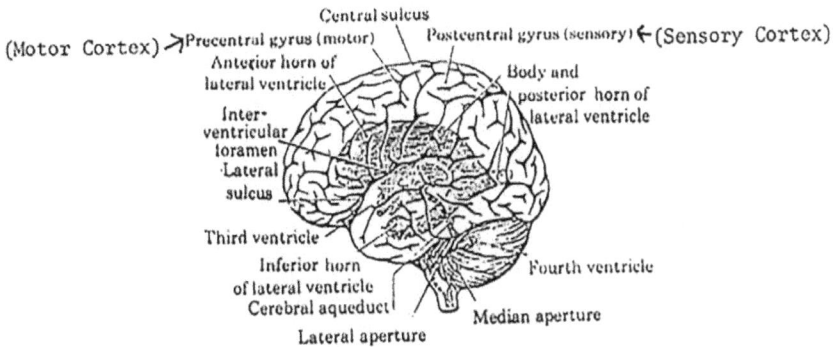

Figure C A view of the Third and Lateral Ventricles in context of Associated Brain Structure

From Bentov, Stalking the Wild Pendulum cortex on the right side of the brain. As a result, according to Bentov, these waves "will stimulate and eventually 'polarize' the cortex in such a way that it will tend to conduct a signal along the homunculus, starting from the toes and on up." The Bentov bio-medical model, as described in a book by Lee Sannella, M.D., entitled: Kundalini-Psychosis or Transcendence, states that the standing acoustical waves are the result of the altered rhythm of heart sounds which are occasioned by prolonged practice of meditation, and which set up sympathetic vibrations in the walls of the fluid filled cavities which comprise the third and lateral ventricles of the brain. In addition, according to Bentov: "The states of bliss described by those whose Kundalini symptoms have completed the full loop along the hemispheres may be explained as a self-stimulation of the pleasure centers in the brain caused by the circulation of a 'current' along the sensory cortex." Bentov also notes, "that most of the described symptoms start on the left side of the body means that it is mostly a development occurring in the right hemisphere." Although normally a period of meditation involving intense concentration and practice for five years or some is required to "bring up the Kundalini," Bentov states that exposure to mechanical or acoustical vibrations in the range of 4-7 Hertz(cycles per second) for protracted periods may achieve the same effect. Bentov cites as an example "repeated riding in a car whose suspension and seat combination produce that range of vibrations, or being exposed for long periods of time to these frequencies caused, for instance, by an air conditioning duct." He also notes that: "The cumulative effect of these vibrations may be able to trigger a spontaneous physio-Kundalini sequence in susceptible people who have a particularly sensitive nervous system."

## 4. Biofeedback.

The third consciousness altering methodology which will be briefly described is biofeedback. Biofeedback is somewhat unique in that it actually employs the self-cognitive powers of the left hemisphere to gain access to such areas of the right brain as the lower cerebral, motor and sensory cortices and assorted pain or pleasure centers. Instead of suppressing the left hemisphere as is done in hypnosis, or largely bypassing and ignoring it as is done in transcendental meditation, biofeedback teaches the left hemisphere first to visualize the desired result and then to recognize the feelings associated with the experience of successful right hemisphere access to the specific lower cerebral, cortex, pain or pleasure or other areas in the manner needed to produce the desired result. Special self-monitoring devices such as the digital thermometer are used to inform the left brain when it succeeds in keying the right hemisphere into accessing the appropriate area. Once this is done, the left brain can then repeatedly instruct the right brain to reestablish the pathways involved so as to produce the same external, objective measures of success. In this way, the pathways are strengthened and emphasized to such an extent that left brain consciousness is enabled to access appropriate areas in the right brain using a conscious, demand mode. For example, if the subject wishes to increase the circulation in the left leg in order to speed up healing he may concentrate with his left brain on achieving that result while carefully monitoring a digital thermometer connected to the left leg. When the concentrated effort begins to achieve success, the digital thermometer will register an increase in the temperature of the left leg. At that point, the subject can mentally (left brain) associate the sensations experienced with the result achieved and can begin to emphasize, by memory recall, the same process to cause its strengthening by affirmation and repetition. In this way, pain can be blocked, healing can be enhanced, malignant tumors can apparently be suppressed and ultimately destroyed, the body's pleasure centers can be stimulated, and a variety of specific physiological results may be achieved. In addition, biofeedback may be used to greatly accelerate achievement of deep meditative states particularly for beginners who have no experience in meditative techniques and whose progress in that methodology is enhanced through effective visualization and external, objective affirmation. Display of the subject's brainwave pattern on a cathode ray tube has proven to be a laboratory-validated means by which subjects may quickly learn to place themselves in profoundly relaxed states characterized by the sort of quietude and singularity of mental focus associated with advanced meditation.

## 5. Gateway and Hemi-Sync.

Now that we have briefly profiled the basic mechanics of the principal techniques for altering or expanding consciousness which share some of the objectives and/or methods employed in the Gateway Experience, we may proceed to focus on what that technique actually involves. Fundamentally, the Gateway Experience is a training system designed to bring enhanced strength, focus and coherence to the amplitude and frequency of brainwave output between the left and right hemispheres so as to alter consciousness, moving it outside the physical sphere so as to ultimately escape even the restrictions of time and space. The participant then gains access to the various levels of intuitive knowledge which the universe offers. What differentiates the Gateway Experience from forms of meditation is its use of the Hemi-Sync technique which is defined in a monograph by Monroe Institute trainer Melissa Jager as, "a state of consciousness defined when the EEG patterns of both hemispheres are simultaneously equal in amplitude and frequency." Although Hemi-Sync seems to be rather rare and of only short duration in ordinary human consciousness, Melissa Jager states that: "Audio techniques developed by Bob Monroe can induce and sustain Hemi-Sync with the Institute's basic Focus 3 tapes,..." She also notes that: "Studies conducted by Elmer and Alyce Greene at the Menninger Foundation have shown that a subject with 20 years of training in Zen meditation could consistently establish Hemi-Sync at will, sustaining it for over 15 minutes." Dr. Stuart Twemlow, a psychiatrist and a research associate of the Monroe Institute, reports that: "In our studies of the effect of the Monroe tape system on brainwaves, we have found that the tapes encourage the focusing of brain energy(it can be measured as with a lightbulb, in watts) into a narrower and narrower 'frequency band'. This focusing of energy is not unlike the yoga concept of one pointedness, which we may translate in western terms as a Single-mindedness." Dr. Twemlow goes on to observe that as the individual gets into the tapes beyond Focus 3, "...there is a gradual increase in brainwave size which is a measure of brain energy or power."

## 6. Lamp vs Laser:

Melissa Jager uses a metaphor to help clarify the process involved in the use of Hemi-Sync in the Gateway Experience. She points out that the human mind in its natural state may be likened to an ordinary lamp which expends energy in the form of both heat and light but in a chaotic, incoherent way which diffuses its energy over a wide area of rather limited depth. On the other hand, the human mind under the discipline of Hemi-Sync acts after the fashion of a laser beam which produces a disciplined stream of light. The stream of energy is projected with total coherence of both frequency and amplitude such that the surface area of a laser beam contains billions of times the concentrated energy found in a similar surface area on the sun. Gateway assumes that once the frequency and amplitude of the human brain are rendered coherent, it is possible to begin accelerating both so that the human mind is soon resonating at ever higher vibrational levels. The mind can then bring itself into synchronization with more sophisticated and rarified energy levels in the universe. The mind, when operating at these increasingly rarified levels is assumed to be capable of processing the information thus received through the same fundamental matrix by which it makes sense of ordinary physical sensory input to achieve meaning in a cognitive context. Such meaning is usually perceived visually in the form of symbols but may also be perceived as astonishing flashes of holistic intuition or even in the form of scenarios involving both visual and aural perception. The mechanics by which the mind exercises the consciousness function will be addressed in more detail later in this paper.

## *7. Frequency Following Response.*

To achieve synchronization of brain hemispheres, the Hemi-Sync technique takes advantage of a phenomenon known as the Frequency Following Response(FFR) which means that if a subject hears a sound produced at a frequency which emulates one of those associated with the operation of the human brain, the brain will try to mimic the same frequency pattern by adjusting its brainwave output. Therefore, if the subject is in a fully awake state but hears sound frequencies which approximates brainwave output at the Theta level, the subject's brain will endeavor to alter its brainwave pattern from the normal Beta to the Theta level. Since the Theta level is associated with sleep, the subject concerned may progress from a fully awake to a sleep state(provided that he does not consciously resist) as the brain strives to entrain its wave frequency output with the one which the person hears. Since these brainwave frequencies are outside the spectrum of sounds which can be heard in pure form by the human ear, Hemi-Sync must produce them based on another phenomenon known as the brain's capacity for deducing "beat" frequencies. If the human brain is exposed to one frequency in the left ear which is 10 Hertz below another audible frequency played in the right ear, rather than hearing either of the two audible frequencies, the brain chooses to "hear" the difference between them, the "beat" frequency. Thus, availing itself of the FFR phenomenon, and using the technique of "beat" frequencies, the Gateway system uses Hemi-Sync and other audio techniques employing the FFR phenomenon to introduce a variety of frequencies which are played at a virtually subliminal, marginally audible level. The objective is to relax the left hemisphere of the brain, place the physical body in a virtual sleep state, and bring the left and right hemispheres into coherence under conditions designed to promote the production of ever higher amplitude and frequency of brainwave output. Audible and perhaps subliminal suggestions by Bob Monroe accompany the various brainwave frequencies, which are sometimes rolled in together with other sounds such as sea surf to mask the sound frequencies where desirable. In this way, Gateway endeavors to provide the subject with the tools by which he may alter his consciousness based on his own volition over time through the repetitive use of the tapes so as to access, via intuitive means, new categories of information not available to ordinary consciousness.

## 8. Role of Resonance.

However, brain coherence through entrainment to "beat" frequencies introduced via stereo headphones is only part of the reason why the Gateway system works. It is also designed to achieve the physical quietude characteristic of deep transcendental meditative states which brings about a complete alteration of the fundamental resonance pattern associated with the sound frequencies produced by the human body. Yoga, zen or transcendental meditation, if practiced long enough, will produce a change in the sound frequency with which the human heart resonates throughout the entire body. According to Bentov, this change in resonance results from elimination of what the medical profession calls "the bifurcation echo" so that the sound of the heartbeat can move synchronously up and down the circulatory system in harmonious resonance approximately seven times a second. Bentov describes the roll played by the bifurcation echo as follows: "When the left ventricle of the heart ejects blood, the aorta, being elastic, balloons out just beyond the valve and causes a pressure pulse to travel down along the aorta. When the pressure pulse reaches the bifurcation in the lower abdomen (which is where the aorta forks in two to go into the legs), part of the pressure pulse rebounds and starts traveling up the aorta. If in the meantime the heart ejects more blood, and a new pressure pulse is traveling down, these two pressure points will eventually collide somewhere along the aorta and produce an interference pattern." By placing the body in a sleeplike state, the Gateway tapes achieve the same goal as meditation in that it places the body in such a profoundly relaxed state that the bifurcation echo slowly fades away as the heart lessens the force and frequency with which it pushes blood into the aorta. The result is a regular, rhythmic sinewave pattern of sound which echoes throughout the body and rises up into the head in sustained resonance. The amplitude of this sinewave pattern, when measured with a sensitive, seismograph type instrument is about three times the average of the sound volume produced by the heart when it is operating normally.

## 9. Brain Stimulation.

Bentov's biomedical model shows that this resonance is of considerable importance since it is directly transmitted to and impacts upon the
brain. The resulting vibration is received and transmitted into the brain
itself via the fluid filled third and left ventricles located above the brain
stem. An electromagnetic pulse is then generated which stimulates the
brain to raise the amplitude and frequency of brainwave output, just as
Dr. Twemlow observed in his research on the effects of the Hemi-Sync
tapes. Also, the brain is contained in a tight membrane called the dura
which is, in turn, cushioned by a thin layer of fluid located between it
and the skull. As the coherent resonance produced by the human heart
in a state of profound relaxation reaches the fluid layer surrounding the
brain, it sets up a rhythmic pattern in which the brain moves up and down
approximately 0.005 to 0.010 millimeters in a continuous pattern. The
selfreinforcing character of resonant behavior accounts for the body's ability to sustain this movement despite the minimal level of energy involved.
In this way, the entire body, based on its own micromotion, functions as
a tuned vibrational system which transfers energy in a range of between
6.8 and 7.5 Hertz into the earth's ionospheric cavity, which itself resonates
at about 7-7.5 Hertz. Of this process, Bentov states:

"This is occurring at a very long wavelength of about 40,000 Km,
or just about the perimeter of the planet. In other words, the signal
from the movement of our bodies will travel around the world in about
one seventh of a second through the electrostatic field in which we are
imbedded. Such a long wavelength knows no obstacles, and its strength
does not attenuate much over large distances. Naturally it will go through
just about anything: metal, concrete, water, and the fields making up our
bodies. It is the ideal medium for conveying a telepathic signal."

Consequently, the Gateway process is designed to rather rapidly
induce a state of profound calm within the nervous system and to sig-
nificantly lower blood pressure to cause the circulatory system, skeleton
and all other physical organ systems to begin vibrating coherently at
approximately 7-7.5 cycles per second. The resulting resonance sets up a
regular, repetitive sound wave which propagates in consonance with the
electrostatic field of the earth.

## 10. Energy Entrainment.

As the body is turned into a coherent oscillator vibrating in harmony with the surrounding electrostatic medium, the specific exercises included in the Gateway tapes enjoin the participant to build up the energy field surrounding his body, presumably by using energy from the earth's field which the body is now entraining because of its ability to resonate with it. This puts the body's energy field into homogeneity with its surrounding environment and promotes movement of the seat of consciousness into the surrounding environment partly in response to the fact that the two electromagnetic medians are now a single energy continuum. Thus, the same process which moves the brain into focused coherence at steadily higher levels of frequency and amplitude so as to entrain analogous frequencies in the universe for data collection also promotes enhancement of bodily energy levels to a point adequate to permit the subject to experience an out-of-body movement when he is ready to do so(more will be said about this topic later). In addition, by resonating with the earth's electromagnetic sphere the human body creates a surprisingly powerful carrier wave to assist the mind in communication activity with other human minds similarly tuned.

## *11. Consciousness and Energy.*

Before our explanation can proceed any further, it is essential to define the mechanism by which the human mind exercises the function known as consciousness, and to describe the way in which that consciousness operates to deduce meaning from the stimuli which it receives. To do this, we will first consider the fundamental character of the material world in which we have our physical existence in order to accurately perceive the raw stuff with which our consciousness must work. The first point which needs to be made is that the two terms, matter and energy tend to be misleading if taken to indicate two distinctly different states of existence in the physical world that we know it. Indeed, if the term matter is taken to mean solid substance as opposed to energy which is understood to mean a force of some sort, then the use of the former is entirely misleading. Science now knows that both the electrons which spin in the energy field located around the nucleus of the atom and the nucleus itself are made up of nothing more than oscillating energy grids. Solid matter, in the strict construction of the term, simply does not exist. Rather, atomic structure is composed of oscillating energy grids surrounded by other oscillating energy grids which orbit at extraordinarily high speeds. In his book, Stalking the Wild Pendulum, Itzhak Bentov gives the following figures. The energy grid which composes the nucleus of the atom vibrates at approximately 1022 Hertz(which means 10 followed by 22 zeros). At 70 degrees Farenheit an atom oscillates at the rate of 1015 Hertz. An entire molecule, composed of a number of atoms bound together in a single energy field vibrates in the range of 109 Hertz. A live human cell vibrates at approximately 103 Hertz. The point to be made is that the entire human being, brain, consciousness and all is, like the universe which surrounds him, nothing more or less than an extraordinarily complex system of energy fields. The so called states of matter are actually variances in the state of energy, and human consciousness is a function of the interaction of energy in two opposite states(motion vs rest) in a manner described in the following paragraph.

## *12. Holograms.*

Energy creates, stores and retrieves meaning in the universe by projecting or expanding at certain frequencies in a three dimensional mode that creates a living pattern called a hologram. The concept of the hologram can be most easily understood by using an example cited by Bentov in which he asks the reader to visualize a bowl full of water into which three pebbles are dropped. As the ripples created by the simultaneous entry of the three pebbles radiate outward towards the rim of the bowl, Bentov further asks the reader to visualize that the surface of the water is suddenly flash frozen so that the ripple pattern is preserved instantly. The ice is removed leaving the three pebbles still laying at the bottom of the bowl. Then the ice is exposed to a powerful, coherent source of light, such as a laser. The result will be a three dimensional model or representation of the position of the three pebbles suspended in midair. Holograms are capable of encoding so much detail that, for example, it is possible to take a holographic projection of a glass of swamp water and view it under magnification to see small organisms not visible to the naked eye when the glass of water itself is examined. The whole concept of holography, despite its scientific implications, has only been known to the physicist since the underlying mathematical principles were worked out by Dennis Gabor in 1947(he later won a Nobel Prize for his work). Laboratory demonstration of Gabor's work only occurred years later following invention of the laser. As biologist Lyall Watson explains:

"The purest kind of light available to us is that produced by a laser, which sends out a beam in which all the waves are of one frequency, like those made by an ideal pebble in a perfect pond. When two laser beams touch, they produce an interference pattern of light and dark ripples that can be recorded on a photographic plate. And if one of the beams, instead of coming directly from the laser, is reflected first off an object such as a human face, the resulting pattern will be very complex indeed, but it can still be recorded. The record will be a hologram of the face."

## 13. *The Part Encodes the Whole.*

Of further importance is the fact that even if we dropped our frozen hologram of the ripple pattern on the floor and broke it into a number of pieces each individual piece would recreate the entire holographic image all by itself. The smaller the piece, the fuzzier and more distorted would be the resulting holographic projection but the fact remains that a whole projection would nonetheless be made. The key to creating any hologram is that energy in motion must interact with energy in a state of rest(nonmotion). In the foregoing example, the pebbles represent energy in motion while the water(before its agitation by the pebbles) represents energy at a state of rest. To activate or, in effect, to "perceive" the meaning of a holograph, energy(in this case, a coherent light source such as a laser beam) must be passed through the interference pattern generated by interaction between the moving energy and the energy at rest. In the simple example given by Bentov, this requirement was fulfilled by holding the frozen interference pattern in front of the coherent light to project the three dimensional holographic image(its "meaning") into space. As Marilyn Ferguson, editor of the Brain/Mind Bulletin tells us:

"Another Feature of a hologram is its efficiency. Billions of bits of information can be stored in a tiny space. The pattern of the holographic photograph]...is stored everywhere on the plate."

## 14. *The Consciousness Matrix.*

The universe is composed of interacting energy fields, some at rest and some in motion. It is, in and of itself, one gigantic hologram of unbelievable complexity. According to the theories of Karl Pribram, a neuroscientist at Stanford University and David Bohm, a physicist at the University of London, the human mind is also a hologram which attunes itself to the universal hologram by the medium of energy exchange thereby deducing meaning and achieving the state which we call consciousness. With respect to states of expanded or altered consciousness such as Gateway uses, the process operates in the following way. As energy passes through various aspects of the universal hologram and is perceived by the electrostatic fields which comprise the human mind, the holographic images being conveyed are projected upon those electrostatic fields of the mind and are perceived or understood to the extent that the electrostatic field is operating at a frequency and amplitude that can harmonize with and therefore "read" the energy carrier wave pattern passing through it. Changes in the frequency and amplitude of the electrostatic field which comprises the human mind determines the configuration and hence the character of the holographic energy matrix which the mind projects to intercept meaning directly from the holographic transmissions of the universe. Then, to make sense of what the holographic image is "saying" to it, the mind proceeds to compare the image just received with itself. Specifically, it does this by comparing the image received with that part of its own hologram which constitutes memory. By registering differences in geometric form and in energy frequency, the consciousness perceives(see Exhibit 2, next page). As psychologist Keith Floyd puts it:

"Contrary to what everyone knows is so, it may not be the brain that produces consciousness--but rather, consciousness that creates the appearance of the brain..."

## 15. Brain in phase:

The consciousness process is most easily envisaged if we picture the holographic input with a three dimensional grid system superimposed over it such that all of the energy patterns contained within can be described in terms of three dimensional geometry using mathematics to reduce the data to two dimensional form. Bentov states that scientists suspect that the human mind operates on a simple binary "go/no go" system as do all digital computers. Therefore, once it superimposes a three dimensional matrix over holographic information it wishes to interpret and reduces that information mathematically to two dimensional form, it can completely process it using its fundamental binary system just as any computer made by the hand of man can process volumes of data and make various comparisons between the data and information stored in its digital memory. Our minds operate in the same way, perceiving by comparison only. Bentov states the proposition this way: "Our whole reality is constructed by constantly making such comparisons....Whenever we perceive something, we always perceive differences only." In states of expanded consciousness, the right hemisphere of the human brain in its holistic, nonlinear and nonverbal mode of functioning acts as the primary matrix or receptor for this holographic input while, by operating in phase or coherence with the right brain, the left hemisphere provides the secondary matrix through its binary, computer-like method of functioning to screen further the data by comparison and reduce it to a discreet, two dimensional form.

## 16. Evaluation.

To the extent that Gateway succeeds in bringing about a refinement in energy matrix of the mind, it succeeds in expanding or altering human consciousness so that it can perceive without recourse to the intercession of the physical senses such that ever more of the universal hologram(not, of course, accessible by sense perception) can ultimately be perceived and understood. Marilyn Ferguson has written that the theories of Pribram and Bohm "appear to account for all transcendental experience, paranormal events and even "normal" perceptual oddities..." She goes on to say of Pribram:

"Currently he is proposing a startling, all-encompassing model that is generating considerable excitement among those intrigued by the mysteries of human consciousness. His "holographic model" marries brain research to theoretical physics; it accounts for normal perception and simultaneously takes the paranormal and transcendental experiences out of the supernatural by explaining them as a part of nature.

Like certain strange discoveries of quantum physics, the radical reorientation of this theory suddenly makes sense of paradoxical sayings of mystics throughout the ages."

## *17. Self Cognition.*

To complete our outline of the process by which the mind achieves and exercises consciousness, we must also describe the mechanism which accounts for the aspect of human thought that differentiates it from the consciousness of plants or animals, i.e. self cognition. Humans not only know, but they know that they know. They are able to monitor the process of their own thinking and maintain an awareness of it. Moreover, they can conduct a comparitive

The Functions of Brain Hemispheres in Consciousness

CONSCIOUSNESS ENERGY GRID

Left Hemisphere
Consciousness Grid

Acts like the Mind's computer software to reduce input from right hemisphere to verbal symbols and concepts

Right Hemisphere
Consciousness Grid

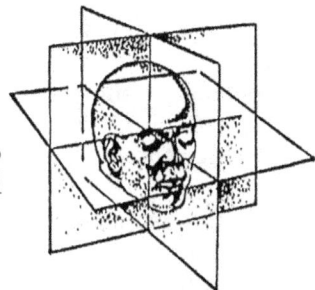

EXHIBIT 2

Reduces three dimensional holographic image to two dimensional go/no go focus

assessment, evaluating the functioning of their thought processes against various "objective" standards they have adopted. Human consciousness can do this because it has the capacity to duplicate aspects of its own hologram, project them out, "perceive" that projection, put it through comparison with the memory aspect(where its evaluation standards of measure are stored) of its own hologram, and measure or "sense" the differences using three dimensional geometry and then binary "go/no go" pulse to yield verbal cognition about the self.

## 18. Time-Space Dimension.

Up to this point our discussion of the Gateway process has been relatively simple and easy to follow. Now the fun begins. Gateway involves more than just perception of those aspects of the universal hologram which can be accessed in the dimension of time-space as we know it. To explain how and why human consciousness can be brought to transcend the limitations of time-space is the next task which must be addressed. To do this we must first appreciate what time and space are in order to understand how the dimension that they constitute can be transcended. Physicists define time as a measurement of energy of force in motion. In other words, it is a measurement of change. However, in order for energy to be in motion it must first be limited in some way within the confines of some sort of vibratory pattern so that its confinement gives it the capacity for being contained at a specific location which is distinguishable from other locations(space). Energy which is not confined is force without limit, without dimension, without the limits of form. It is infinity, cannot move because there is nothing beyond infinity, and is therefore outside of the dimension of time.

It is also beyond space because that concept implies that a specific energy form is limited to a specific location, and is absent from other locations. But if energy is in the state of infinity, there are no boundaries, no "here" to differentiate from "there", no sense of area. Energy in infinity means energy uniformly extended without limit. It has no beginning, no end, no location. It is conscious force, the fundamental, primal power of existence without form, a state of infinite being. Energy in infinity is said to be completely at rest and, therefore, cannot generate holograms so long as it remains utterly inactive. It retains its inherent capacity for consciousness in that it can receive and passively perceive holograms generated by energy in motion out in the various dimensions which make up the created universe put it cannot be perceived by consciousness operating in the active universe. Energy in this state of inactive infinity is termed by physicists as energy in its absolute state, or simply "the Absolute." Between the Absolute and the "material" universe in which we experience our physical existence are various intervening dimensions to which human consciousness in altered states of being may gain access. Theoretically, human consciousness may continue to expand the horizons of its perceptual capability until it reaches the dimension of the Absolute at which point perception stops because the Absolute generates no holograms of or about itself.

## 19. Intervening dimensions.

Since the Absolute is conscious energy in infinity(i.e. without boundaries), it occupies every dimension to include the time-space dimension in which we have our physical existence but we cannot perceive it. It overlays everything as do many of the intervening gradients or dimensions through which the energies of the universe pass on their way to and from their home in the state of infinity(the absolute). To enter these intervening dimensions, human consciousness must focus with such intense coherence that the frequency of the energy pattern which comprises that consciousness(i.e. the brainwave output) can accelerate to the point where the resulting frequency pattern, if displayed on an oscilloscope, would look virtually like a solid line. Achievement of this state of altered consciousness sets the stage for perception of non-time-space dimensions because of the operation of a principle in physics known as Planck's Distance.

This is an aspect of quantum mechanics which applies to the fact that any oscillating frequency(such as a brainwave) reaches two points of complete rest which constitute the boundaries of each individual oscillation(i.e. movement up or down). Without these points of rest, an oscillating wave pattern would be impossible since the points of rest are required to permit the energy to change direction and thus continue vibrating between rigid limits. But it is also true that when, for an infinitesimally brief instant, that energy reaches one of its two points of rest it "clicks out" of time-space and joins infinity(see Exhibit 3, next page). That critical step out of time-space occurs when the speed of the oscillation drops below 10-33 centimeters per second(Planck's Distance). To use the words of Bentov: "...quantum mechanics tell us that when distances go below Planck's Distance, which is 10-33 CM, we enter, in effect, a new world." To return to our case in point, the human consciousness wave pattern reaches such high frequency that the pattern of "clickouts" comes so close together that there is virtual continuity in it. Then, a portion of that consciousness is actually postulated to establish and maintain its information collection function in those dimensions located between time-space and the Absolute. Thus, as the almost continuous "clickout" pattern establishes itself in continuous phase at speeds below Planck's

Distance but before reaching the state of total rest, human consciousness passes through the looking glass of time-space after the fashion of
Alice beginning her journey into wonderland. The Gateway experience,
with its associated Hemi-Sync technique, is apparently designed, if used
systematically and patiently, to enable human consciousness to establish
a coherent pattern of perception in those dimensions where speeds
below Planck's distance apply. This holds true irrespective of whether the
individual is exercising his consciousness while in his physical body or
whether he is doing so after having separated that consciousness from
the physical body(i.e. the so called out-of-body state mentioned earlier).

## 20. Subatomic Particles.

The behavior of subatomic particles provides an interesting example
of the phenomenon of "clicking out" discussed in the preceding para-
graphs. In an article prepared for Science Digest magazine, Dr. John
Gliedman mentions the way in which subatomic particles communicate
with each other once their energy fields become entrained as a result of
colliding with each other. The communication concerned is, of course,
postulated to be occurring during the "click out phase" in the oscillation
of the energy fields comprising the subatomic particles concerned. It is
this cause which accounts for the cross-communication at what in terms
of time-space velocities, would seem to involve speeds in excess of light. In
reality Einstein's Theory of Relativity is not being invalidated but, rather,
the communication concerned is taking place outside the dimension of
time-space to which the Theory of Relativity is strictly confined. Specifically, Dr. Gleidman tells us: "Quantum theory postulates a kind of long
range Siamese twin effect whenever two subatomic particles collide and
then go their different ways. Even when the particles are halfway across
the universe from each other, it says, they instantaneously respond to each
other's actions. And in so doing, they violate relativity's ban on faster than
light velocities." Indeed, regarding attempts to quantify what is known
about the behavior of energy in dimensions apparently outside of time-
space, Bentov speaks about, "...courageous physicists who are working on
hypothetical particles, called 'tachyons,' which can move at speeds higher
than light. The speed of tachyons starts just above the speed of light and
ranges all the way to infinite velocities."

## 21. Dimensions In-between.

Now that we have postulated the legitimacy of the assertion that the
energy forms which compose consciousness can move beyond the time-
space dimension, we need to turn our attention to the energy forms which

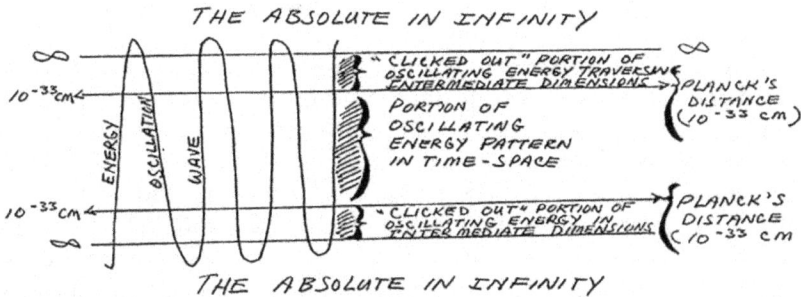

THE ABSOLUTE IN INFINITY

"CLICKED OUT" PORTION OF OSCILLATING ENERGY TRAVERSING INTERMEDIATE DIMENSIONS → PLANCK'S DISTANCE ($10^{-33}$ cm)

PORTION OF OSCILLATING ENERGY PATTERN IN TIME-SPACE

"CLICKED OUT" PORTION OF OSCILLATING ENERGY IN INTERMEDIATE DIMENSIONS → PLANCK'S DISTANCE ($10^{-33}$ cm)

THE ABSOLUTE IN INFINITY

**EXHIBIT 3**

Graphical Display of the "Click Out" Phenomenon

From Bentov, Stalking the Wild Pendulum.

inhabit those dimensions between time-space and the Absolute. In so doing, we may better perceive the form that "reality" assumes when we encounter it in those intermediate dimensions. In this context, Bentov tells us that:

"The causal relationship between events breaks down; movements become jerky rather than smooth. Time and space may become "grainy" or "chunky." Perhaps a piece of space can be traversed by a particle of matter in any direction without necessarily being synchronized with a piece of time. In short, a pair of events will occur in either time or space, the pair not being connected causally but by a random fluctuation."

What Bentov means is that inside the dimension of time-space where both concepts apply in a generally uniform way there is a proportional relationship between them. A certain space can be covered by energy moving in either particle or wave form in a certain time assuming a specific velocity virtually anywhere in the time-space universe. The relationship is neat and predictable. However, in the intermediate dimensions beyond time-space the limitations imposed on energy to put it into a state of oscillating motion are not uniform as they are in our physical universe. A myriad of various distortions and incongruities are thus likely to be encountered such that our nice neat assumptions concerning the relationship between time and space as we know it in this dimension do not apply. But even more important, access is opened to both the past and the future when the dimension of current time-space is left behind.

## 22. Special Status, Out-of-Body Experience.

Although human consciousness can, with enough practice, move beyond the dimension of time-space and interface with other energy systems in other dimensions, the entire process is appreciably enhanced if that consciousness can be detached in large measure from the physical body before such interface is attempted. Once an individual becomes proficient in the technique of out-of-body movement and then reaches the point where he is able to break out of time-space while out of his body, he gains the advantage of "clicking out" part of his enhanced consciousness while starting from a base located much closer to the dimensions with which he wishes to communicate. In other words, since he is starting from a point much "higher up", to use an analogy from the time-space context, that part of his consciousness involved in "clicking out" will have that much more time to interact in dimensions beyond time-space because less time is required to traverse the intervening layers.

Moreover, once the individual is able to project his consciousness beyond time-space, that consciousness would logically tend to entrain its frequency output with the new energy environment to which it is exposed, therein greatly enhancing the extent to which the individual's altered consciousness may be further modified to achieve a much heightened point of focus and a much refined oscillating pattern. As a result, a self-reinforcing process should ensue whereby the farther consciousness in the out-of-body state can be projected beyond the time-space dimension, the more its level of energy output would be enhanced, thus promoting the potential for still further travel. The tentative conclusion to be drawn is that the out-of-body state may be regarded as an extremely effective way of accelerating the process of enhancing consciousness and of interfacing with dimensions beyond time-space. If the practitioner of the Gateway technique has a choice of concentrating on achieving and exploiting the out-of-body experience as opposed to concentrating his full efforts on expanding his consciousness exclusively from a physical base, the former would appear to promise much faster and more impressive successes than does the latter.

## 23. Absolute in Perspective.

It may be helpful at this point to pause and recap the major aspects of our intellectual journey from time-space to the realm of the Absolute. We have spoken at some length concerning the incredibly complex hologram which is created by the intersection of energy patterns generated by the totality of all dimensions of the universe, time-space included. We have noted that our minds constitute energy fields which interact with various aspects of this hologram to deduce information which is ultimately processed through the left hemisphere of our brains to reduce it to a form that we employ for the process we call thinking. We have implied that this hologram is the finite embodiment in active, energy form of the infinite consciousness of the Absolute. It is the title we assigned to that vast pool of energy in a state of perfect rest over which the physical universe is layered, and from whence it comes. Incidentally, to describe this, Bentov uses the analogy of a very deep sea, comparing the still depths of the sea to the dimension of the Absolute while assigning the storm-tossed waves above to represent the physical universe with which we are familiar. The slightly agitated currents of the sea to be found in between the turbulent surface and the totally still depths represent energy in the process of either going into rest(i.e. approaching infinity) or coming out of rest.

## 24. From Big Bang to Torus.

Working from the widely accepted "Big Bang" theory Bentov presents a conceptual model to depict the process of time-space evolution the relative position of the universal hologram. That hologram is often called a "Torus" because it is thought to have the overall shape of an immense, self-contained spiral. Basing his thesis on recent studies concerning the distribution of quasars(quasi-stellar objects), and operating on the premise that in the universe smaller processes tend to be mirror images of larger ones(i.e. the pattern of electrons around the nucleus of an atom mirrors the way planets orbit their suns, and so on) Bentov postulates the following scenario. Taking his cue from the observed capability of quasars to eject enormously concentrated beams of matter from their interiors in a controlled, non-concentric version of the "Big-bang" he envisages a similar process occurring in the generation of the universe(see Exhibit 4, next page).

Noting that those galaxies located to the north of our own galaxy are moving away faster than those located to the south, and that those to the east and west are demonstrably more distant, Bentov regards this as substantive evidence that the jet of matter which expanded into our universe has turned back upon itself, eventually forming an ovoid or egg shape. He sees "matter" in our universe entering the ovoid pattern following ejection from a nucleus composed of extremely compressed energy through a "white hole." At the end of its trip to the far end of the ovoid, he sees it departing via a "black hole". In such a model, time is observed to be a measure of the change which occurs as energy evolves into new, more complex forms as it progresses along the distance from the white hole side of the nucleus, around the shell of this "cosmic egg" until it enters the black hole. In other words, as energy--expelled from infinity and confined within limits by the conscious of the Absolute--achieves form and motion following ejection from the white hole at the top of the egg, time begins as a measure of the cadence of this evolutionary movement as "reality" goes around the shell of the egg on its journey to the black hole at the far end.

## 25. Our Place in Time.

The observed distribution of galaxies suggests that our particular universe is located near the top of the egg at the point where matter begins to fall back on itself, thus explaining the reason why the galaxies to the north are seen to be moving away more rapidly as they are caught up in the downturn of the stream of matter towards the far end of the cosmic egg(see Exhibit 5, next page). Layered over this cosmic egg is the Absolute which sustains the radiating nucleus from which the original jet of matter issued forth. As the stream of matter moves around the ovoid towards its destination at the black hole where it

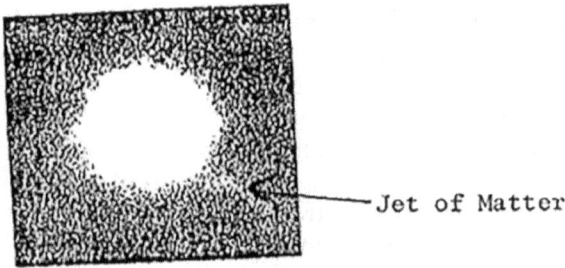

Figure A Photograph of Quaser Emitting Jet of Matter

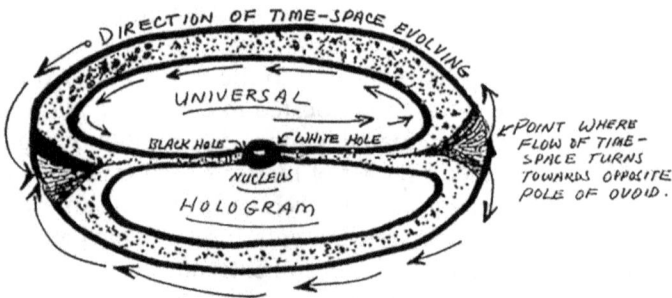

Figure B Diagram of the Cosmic Egg

EXHIBIT 4

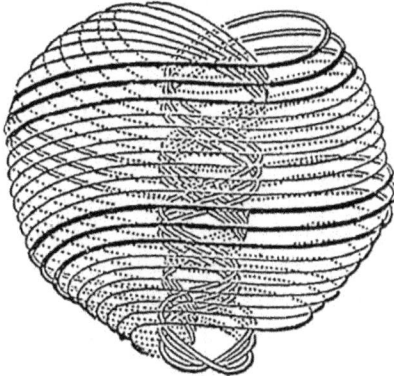

Figure C Stylized Rendition of a Simple Torus

(Figures A and B from Bentov, Stalking the Wild Pendulum, Fig. C, Purce, THE MYSTIC SPIRAL)
Relative Position of Our Galaxy in the Universe

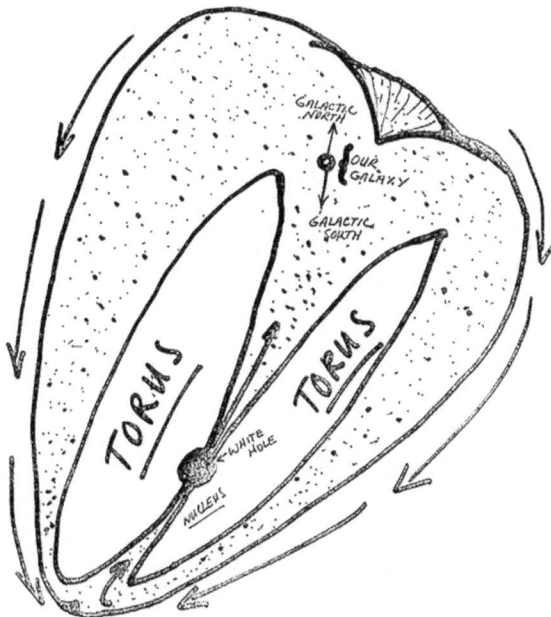

EXHIBIT 5

From Bentov, Stalking the Wild Pendulum.

will be reabsorbed into the radiating nucleus and then the Absolute, it generates the interference pattern within the cosmic egg which constitutes the universal hologram or Torus. Since the Torus is being simultaneously generated by matter in all the various phases of "time", it reflects the development of the universe in the past, present and future(as it would be seen from our particular perspective in one phase of time). By reflecting on this model, it becomes possible to "see" how human consciousness brought to a sufficiently altered(focused) state could obtain information concerning the past, present an future since they all exist in the universal hologram simultaneously(In the case of the future because all of the consequences of the past and present can be seen coming together in the hologram such that the future can be predicted or "seen" with total accuracy). Moreover, it is possible to see how the implosion of energy patterns would cross and recross to create an incredibly complex four dimensional hologram or Torus, in spiral shape in reflection of the multi-dimensional developing pattern of evolution. All of the movements of the energies which comprise the universe leave their mark and hence tell their story throughout time.

## 26. Quality of Consciousness.

We noted earlier that the out-of-body state involves projection of a major portion of the energy pattern that represents human consciousness so that it may move either freely throughout the terrestrial sphere for purposes of information acquisition or into other dimensions outside of time-space, perhaps to interact with other forms of consciousness within the universe. Consciousness is the organizing and sustaining principle that provides the impetus and guidance to bring and keep energy in motion within a given set of parameters so that a specific reality will result. When consciousness reaches a state of sophistication in which it can perceive itself(its own hologram) it reaches the point of selfcognition. Human beings have this form of elevated consciousness as does the Absolute but in case of the latter, it is a function of energy and its associated quality of consciousness in infinity(omniscience and omnipotence in perceptual unity). When energy returns to a state of total rest within the Absolute, it returns to the continuum of consciousness in the pool of limitless, timeless perception that resides there. Thus, the more complex an energy system in the "material" state, the more consciousness it possesses to maintain its reality. Our consciousness, therefore, is that differentiated aspect of the universal consciousness which resides within the Absolute. It accounts for the organization of the energy patterns which constitute our physical body but is distinctly separate from and superior to it. Since consciousness exists quite apart from and outside of reality, beyond the bounds of time-space, it, like the Absolute, has neither beginning nor end. Reality has both a beginning and an end because it is bounded within time-space, but the fundamental quantum of energy and its associated consciousness is eternal. When reality ends, its constituent energy simply returns to infinity in the Absolute.

## *27. Consciousness in Perspective.*

Having ascertained that human consciousness is able to separate from physical reality and interact with other intelligences in other dimensions within the universe, and that it is both eternal and destined for ultimate return to the Absolute we are faced with the question: "So what happens then?" Since memory is a function of consciousness and therefore enjoys the same eternal character as the consciousness which accounts for its existence it must be admitted that when consciousness returns to the Absolute it brings with it all the memories it has accumulated through experience in reality. The return of consciousness to the Absolute does not imply an extinction of the separate entity which the consciousness organized and sustained in reality. Rather, it suggests a differentiated consciousness which merges with and participates in the universal consciousness and infinity of the Absolute without losing the separate identity and accumulated self-knowledge which its memories confer upon it. What it does lose is the capability for generation of independent thought holograms, since that can be done only by energy in motion. In other words, it retains the power to perceive but loses the power of will or choice. In exchange, however, this consciousness participates in the all-knowing infinite continuum of consciousness which is a characteristic of energy in the ever present. Consequently, it is accurate to observe that when a person experiences the out-of- body state he is, in fact, projecting that eternal spark of consciousness and memory which constitutes the ultimate source of his identity to let it play in and learn from dimensions both inside and outside the time-space world in which his physical component currently enjoys a short period of reality.

## *28. Gateway Method.*

Having put the Gateway Experience in context by postulating a structural outline of how and why it seems to work, and having shown what it is designed to achieve, the time has come to examine the specific techniques which comprise the Gateway training process. These techniques are designed to enable the user of the Gateway tapes to manipulate the high energy states which can be achieved if the user continues to work with the tapes over a period of time. The amount of time required to reach advanced energy states and to fully exploit the techniques varies with the individual. The sensitivity of his nervous system, his general state of mind, and the extent to which he may have previously developed facility in related techniques such as transcendental meditation are all pertinent factors affecting the speed at which he may expect to progress. The

Gateway process begins by teaching the individual participant to isolate extraneous concerns in a visualization device called an "energy conversion box." Next, the participant is introduced to a method of encouraging his mind and body to strive to achieve a state of resonance through utterance of a single tone, a monotonous, protracted humming sound that sets up a feeling of vibration particularly in the head. He engages in this "resonate tuning" as it is called by humming along with a chorus of such sounds that are contained on the Gateway tape. Following this, the participant is exposed to the Gateway affirmation, and is encouraged to repeat it to himself as he hears it repeated on the tape. This affirmation is a statement to the effect that the individual realizes that he is more than merely a physical body and that he deeply desires to expand his consciousness.

## 29. Hemi-Sync Introduced.

After that, he is exposed for the first time to the Hemi-Sync sound frequencies, and is encouraged to focus on and develop a perception of and appreciation for those feelings which accompany the synchronization of brainwaves that results. Next comes the technique of progressive and systematic physical relaxation while the Hemi-Sync frequencies are expanded to include additional forms of "pink and white" noise designed to put the physical body at the virtual threshold of sleep as well as to calm the left hemisphere of the mind while raising the right hemisphere to a state of heightened attentiveness. Once all of this is achieved, the participant is invited to envisage creation of an "energy balloon" comprised of an energy flow beginning at the center of the top of the head and extending down in all directions to the feet. The energy involved in this flow then proceeds up through the body and back out into the balloon pattern again. The "energy balloon", which sets up a pattern very reminiscent of the cosmic egg discussed earlier, not only enhances bodily energy flow and encourages early achievement of a suitable resonant state but it is also designed to provide protection against conscious entities possessing lower energy levels which the participant might encounter in the event that he achieves an out-of-body, state. It serves a precautionary purpose in the unlikely event that the participant's first out-of-body experience involves direct projection outside the terrestrial sphere.

## 30. Advanced Techniques.

Having reached Focus 10, the participant is now ready to endeavor to achieve a state of sufficiently expanded awareness to begin actually interacting with dimensions beyond those associated with his experience of physical reality. This state is called Focus 12 and involves conscious efforts on his part while additional forms of "pink and white noise" enter the sound stream being directed into his ears from the Gateway tape. Once the participant has achieved this state of greatly expanded awareness, he is ready to begin employing a series of specific techniques or "tools" as the Monroe Institute characterizes them which enable him to manipulate his newly found expanded awareness to obtain practical, useful feedback of value for promoting self-discovery and personal growth. The specific techniques involved are described individually below.

A. Problem Solving. This technique involves identifying fundamental problems which the individual wishes to see solved, filling his expanded awareness with his perception of these problems and then projecting them out into the universe. In this way, the individual enlists the assistance of what Monroe Institute calls his "higher self", in other words his expanded consciousness, to interact with the universal hologram to obtain the information required to solve the problem. This approach may be used to solve personal difficulties, technical problems in the realm of physics, mathematics, etc., practical administrative problems, and so on. Responses to the problem solving technique may be received almost immediately, but often they come based on developing intuition over the next two to three days. Frequently the response comes in the form of a sudden, holistic perception in which the individual suddenly finds that he simply knows the answer in all of its ramifications and completely in context, sometimes without even being able to put his newly found perception into words, at least initially. In some cases, the response may even arrive in the form of visual symbols which the individual will"see" with his mind while he is in the Focus 12 state and which he will have to interpret after he returns to normal consciousness.

B. Patterning. This technique involves use of the consciousness to achieve desired objectives in the physical, emotional, or intellectual sphere. It involves concentration on the desired objective while in a Focus 12 state, extension of the individual's perception of that objective into the whole expanded consciousness, and its projection into the universe with the intention that the desired objective is already a matter of established achievement which is destined to be realized within the time frame specified. This particular methodology is based on the belief that the thought patterns generated by our consciousness in a state of expanded awareness create holograms which represent the situation we desire to bring about and, in so doing, establish the basis for actual realization of that goal. Once the thought-generated hologram of the sought after objective is established in the universe it becomes an aspect of reality which interacts with the universal hologram to bring about the desired objective which might not, under other circumstances, ever occur. In other words, the technique of patterning recognizes the fact that since consciousness is the source of all reality, our thoughts have the power to influence the development of reality in time-space as it applies to us if those thoughts can be projected with adequate intensity. However, the more complicated the objective sought and the more radically it departs from our current reality, the more time the universal hologram will need to reorient our reality sphere to accommodate our desires. Monroe trainers caution against attempting to force the pace of this process because the individual could succeed in dislocating his existing reality with drastic consequences.

C. Color Breathing. The next technique is called color breathing and is designed to use the expanded awareness and highly focused attentiveness associated with the Focus 12 state to imagine various colors in a particularly intense and vivid manner so as to use them to resonate with and in turn to activate the body's own energies. Fundamentally, in terms of practical application it is a healing technique which is designed to restore the body and to enhance its physical capabilities by balancing, revitalizing and retuning bodily energy flows. It is predicated on the principle that the body's electromagnetic field is capable of altering its resonance pattern so as to entrain energy from the earth's electrostatic field for its own use, The various colors envisaged in the imagination as part of the technique cue the mind as to which frequencies and what specific amplitudes are desired in connection with this entrainment and the subsequent alterations in bodily energy flow patterns. That color has the capacity to affect the human mind is well known, and the effectuality of color in certain kinds of healing is a demonstrable fact. For example, application of an intense blue light to an area of physical tumescence leads to relatively rapid and easily observable reduction in the swelling while red, and to a lesser extent, yellow have quite the opposite effect. However, in the Hemi-Sync application of the technique external light sources are not involved but, rather, the mind is the sole agent of the healing and revitalization.

D. Energy Bar Tool. Magic wands and enchanted scepters have been part of the folklore and occult practices of many cultures. The scepters, staffs and maces carried by monarchs and high priests alike occur with such frequency in the history of bygone eras as to suggest that at the very least these items are aspects of some type of archetypical symbol which the human mind seems to appreciate, perhaps quite subliminally. In any case, the energy bar tool technique involves envisaging a small, intensely pulsating dot of light which the participant charges in his imagination with enormous energy until it is virtually pulsating. The participant then extrudes the dot into the shape of a sparkling, vibrating cylinder of energy which he then uses to channel force from the universe to selected parts of his body for purposes of healing and revitalization.

E. Remote Viewing. In addition, the energy bar tool is used as a portal for initiating a follow-on technique called "remote viewing." In this context, the participant turns his bar of energy into a whirling vortex through which he sends his imagination in search of new and illuminating insights. The apparent purpose of the symbolism involved in the vortex seems to be to cue the subconscious and convey to it instructions as to what the participant wishes to do but in terms of nonverbal symbols which the right hemisphere of the mind is capable of understanding.

F. Living Body Map. This technique provides amplification for application of the energy bar tool as a means of healing specific areas or systems of the human body. The configuration of the participant's body is imagined and then the various major systems such as the nervous and circulatory systems are envisaged in appropriate colors within the confines of the outline being held in the imagination. The energy bar tool is then applied to energizing, balancing and healing in whatever manner the participant desires. In the process, the participant visualizes various streams of colored energy flowing out of the tool into the organ system or area upon which the revitalizing or healing application is being made. Since colors are the result of differing wavelengths of light, which is to say energy at various frequencies, this technique operates on the assumption that as the human body is composed of energy it can be vitalized and healed through the additive application of additional energy provided that the energy is applied in the appropriate form.

G. Focus 15: Travel into the Past. All of the preceding techniques are conducted at the level of expanded awareness known as Focus 12. However, the technique of time travel into the past involves further expansion of consciousness through the inclusion of additional levels of sound on the Hemi-Sync tapes. Some of the sound is probably merely an intensification of the basic Hemi-Sync frequencies, being designed to further modify brainwave frequency and amplitude. Other aspects of the added sound patterns appear to be designed to provide subtle, almost subliminal suggestions to the mind as to what is desired by way of further expanded consciousness so as to support the verbal suggestions and instructions also contained on the tape. Even the instructions are highly symbolic, with time being visualized as a huge wheel in the universe with various spokes each of which gives access to a different part of the participant's past. Focus 15 is a very advanced state and is extremely difficult to achieve. Probably less than five percent of all participants in any given Gateway Experience actually fully achieve the Focus 15 state during the course of the approximately seven days of training. Nonetheless, Monroe Institute trainers affirm that with enough practice, eventually Focus 15 can be achieved. They also state that not only the individual's past history is available for examination by one who has achieved Focus 15 but other aspects of the past with which the individual himself has had no connection may also be accessed.

H. Focus 21: The Future. The last and most advanced of all the Focus states associated with the Gateway training program involves movement outside of the boundaries of time-space as in Focus 15 but with attention to discovering the future rather than the past. The individual who has achieved this state has reached a truly advanced level. Except in unusual circumstances, it is probably not attainable except by those who have conditioned themselves through long application of meditation or by those who have practiced long and hard through use of the Hemi-Sync tapes for a period of months if not years.

## 31. *The Out-of-Body Movement.*

This remarkable phenomenon has been saved for discussion in detail until last because of the interest which it occasions and special circumstances involved in its attainment. Monroe Institute stresses that the Gateway program was not established solely for the purpose of enabling participants to obtain the out-of-body state nor does the program guarantee that most participants will succeed in doing it during the course of the training at the Institute. Only one tape out of the many which make up the Gateway Experience is devoted to the techniques involved in the out-of-body movement. Basically, these techniques are merely designed to make it easier for the individual to achieve the out-of-body state when his brainwave pattern and personal energy levels have reached a point that he is in apparent harmony with his surrounding electromagnetic environment such that he feels that he has reached the threshold where separation is a possibility. To facilitate achieving the out-of-body state, Bob Monroe, the founder of Monroe Institute, is quoted in a recent magazine article as saying that in order to assist the participant the particular Hemi-Sync tape concerned with that technique employs Beta signals of "around 2877.3 CPS."(cycles per second). Since 30 to 40 CPS is considered to be the normal range for Beta brainwave signals(those associated with the wakeful state), it is apparent that the Monroe Institute is convinced that the same heightened state of brainwave frequency output which promotes altered states of consciousness is also an important consideration in assisting in achievement of out-of-body states. The actual techniques employed for separating from the body involve such simple maneuvers as rolling out, lifting out after the fashion of a telephone pole wherein the individual separates in a rigid, headfirst manner(such that he finds himself standing at attention at the foot of his physical body) and sliding out through either end of his body.

## 32. Role of REM Sleep.

It is interesting to note that Bob Monroe informed the Gateway class that finished 7 May 1983 that an ex-trainer of his operating in Charlottesville, Virginia found that he could guarantee out-of-body movements by bringing participants down into a rapid eye movement(REM) state of sleep and then use the Hemi-Sync tape technique. This may well be a function of the fact that most if not all people reputedly go into an out-of-body state during REM sleep. REM sleep is the deepest possible level of ordinary sleep and involves complete disengagement of the body's motor cortex functions from the neck down and nearly complete suppression of consciousness in the left brain hemisphere. The effect of this is to put the body in a state of complete stillness so far as the skeletal muscle structure is concerned, thereby further promoting the state of deep rest needed to eliminate the bifurcation echo. In addition, it leaves the right hemisphere of the brain free to respond to the instructions and suggestions contained on the Gateway tape. However, use of the Hemi-Sync tapes at this point may be less a factor in actually achieving the out-of-body state than it is a matter of focusing the brain enough so that a residual memory of having naturally achieved an out-of-body state is carried into the waking state. Indeed, it may even be postulated that some dreams associated with deep levels of sleep are in fact functions of the same kind of altered consciousness involved in interaction with the universe that plays a role in all of the Focus 12, 15 and 21 states described above.

The difference between those states and the condition of the mind in REM sleep seems to be that the left hemisphere is almost totally disengaged in the latter experience such that memory of what was achieved in the altered states of consciousness cannot usually be retrieved by conscious desire because the left hemisphere has no knowledge of its existence or its location in the right hemisphere. Admittedly, some people can be trained to remember their REM state dreams through intense conditioning in the waking state but even that may be more a function of establishing pathways in the right hemisphere which the left hemisphere can access following reentry into the wakeful state than it is an indication of any specific left hemisphere conscious involvement in the process during REM sleep. In any event, the three apparent conditions required for voluntarily inducing an out-of-body state in most individuals seems to be: (1) achievement of a state of profound quiet in the body such that the bifurcation echo fades and resonance at approximately 7 Hertz is established, (2) synchronization of the two brain hemisphere wave patterns, and (3) subsequent stimulation of the right hemisphere of the mind to attain a state of heightened alertness(which, of course, interferes with brain hemisphere synchronization but not until a sufficient level of enhanced frequency range has first been established to help achieve the out-of-body state).

## 33. Information Collection Potential.

The information acquisition potential associated with the out-of-body state seems to attract the most attention from the standpoint of developing practical applications for the Gateway technique. Unfortunately, although the out-of-body state can apparently be achieved by many people without excessive expenditure of time or effort, the purposes to which it can be put are currently limited by the fact that although individuals in that state may travel anywhere on an instantaneous basis in either the terrestrial or in other spheres, information distortion in the former context remains a major concern. To date, according to one of the trainers at Monroe Institute, numerous experiments have been conducted involving persons moving from one coast to the other in the out-of-body state to read a series of ten computer generated numbers in a university laboratory. Although most have acquired enough of the digits to make clear that their consciousness was present none have ever succeeded in getting all ten correct. This seems to be a function of the fact that physical reality in the present is not the only holographic influence which the individual may encounter in an out-of-body state. There are also energy patterns left by people or events occurring at the same physical site being viewed, but from the past rather than the present. In addition, since thoughts are the product of energy patterns, and energy patterns are reality, it may also be possible that individuals encounter thought forms while in an out-of-body state which mingle with physical reality and are not easily differentiated. Finally, as Melissa Jager writes, there is another potential problem area in the sense that holograms can be viewed pseudoscopically, that is to say inside out or backwards just as well as they can be seen in proper perspective. Some of the distortions occurring may ultimately prove to be traceable to this cause because in the out-of-body state an individual may perceive the holographic energy patterns given off by people or things interacting in time-space reality in a somewhat distorted form.

## 34. Belief System Considerations.

In 1967, Alexandra David-Neel and Llama Yongden wrote a book entitled Secret Oral Teachings in Tibetan Buddhist Sects, from which the following quote is taken:

"The tangible world is movement, say the Masters, not a collection of moving objects, but movement itself. There are no objects "in movement," it is the movement which constitutes the objects which appear to us: They are nothing but movement.

This movement is a continued and infinitely rapid succession of flashes of energy(in Tibetan "tsal" or "shoug"). All objects perceptible to our senses, all phenomena of whatever kind and whatever aspect they may assume, are constituted by a rapid succession of instantaneous events."

The classic description of the universal hologram is to be found in a Hindu sutra which says:

"In the heaven of Indra there is said to be a network of pearls so arranged that if you look at one you see all the others reflected in it."

I have cited this quotation because it shows that the concept of the universe which at least some physicists are now coming to accept is identical in its essential aspects with the one known to the learned elite in selected civilizations and cultures of high attainment in the ancient world. The concept of the cosmic egg, for example, is well known to scholars familiar with the ancient writings of the eastern religions. Nor are the theories presented in this paper at variance with the essential tenets of the Judeo-Christian stream of thought. The concept of visible reality(i.e. the "created" world) as being an emanation of an omnipotent and omniscient divinity who is completely unknowable in his primary state of being. The Absolute at rest in infinity is a concept straight out of Hebrew mystical philosophy. Even the Christian concept of the Trinity shines through the description of the Absolute as presented in this paper.
The description of energy totally at rest, in infinity fits the Christian metaphysical concept of the Father while the infinite self-consciousness resident in that energy providing the motive force of will to bring a portion of that energy into motion to create reality corresponds with the Son. This is so because in order to attain self-consciousness, the consciousness of the Absolute must project a hologram of itself and then perceive it. That hologram is a mirror image of the Absolute in infinity, still exists outside time and space, but is one step removed from the Absolute and is the actual agent of all creation(all reality). And, the eternal thought or concept of self which results from this self-consciousness serves the Absolute as the model around which the evolution of time-space revolves to ultimately attain a reflection of and union with Him. That thought model, which perfectly reflects the essence or "spirit" of the Absolute fits the Christian metaphysical description of the Holy Spirit. Finally, our description of the universal hologram, the Torus of creation and evolution is neither new nor original. Its use as the figure of the universe, of creation developing

in evolution is found in various stylized representations in virtually every religious system of antiquity, whether of eastern or western derivation. Whether its the stylized labyrinth once popular in the Helenic world, the spiralized version of the Hebrew Tree of Life or its Hindu counterpart, or the Chinese Spiral Through The Fourfold Powers, the ultimate meaning is the same. Mystics the world over, it seems, have perceived the universal hologram in the same spiral form and have incorporated that intuitive knowledge in their religious writings from antiquity to the present.

## *35. Left Brain Limitations.*

Twentieth Century physics would seem to be revisiting insights belonging to mankind as far back as written records can take us: The only difference is that Twentieth Century physics is using a left brain, linear, quantitative style of reasoning to approach the same knowledge which the mystics of old apparently acquired in a holistic, intuitional, right brain style. As a tool in the hands of our left brain culture, Gateway would seem to be a promising method for achieving the intuitive, holistic type of interface with the universal hologram needed to provide the context that thinkers like Einstein have sought in their labors to discover a unified field theory in physics. For persons in our profession whose concerns revolve around strategic issues, tactical questions and matters of managerial form and system, access to a new world of intuitive perception and self reflection would seem to offer, in the long term, the means by which to know in a truly objective way. This is so because the self-imposed limitations to balanced perception and objective logic which our cultural and personal psychological subjectivity imposes when we use the strictly left brain thinking style could be offset by the holistic form of perception associated with altered states of consciousness. To the extent that we come to perceive ourselves fully in the context of that portion of the universal hologram which is the reflection of ourselves, to that extent we release ourselves from the prison of subjectivity.

## *36. Self Knowledge.*

It was axiomatic to the mystic philosophers of old that the first step in personal maturity could be expressed in the aphorism: Know thyself." To them, the education of a man undertook, as its primary step, achievement of an introverted focus so that he learned what was within himself before attempting to approach the outside world. They rightly assumed that he could not effectively evaluate and cope with the world until he fully understood his personal psychological balance. The insights being provided by Twentieth Century psychology in this context through the use of various kinds of personality testing seem to be a revalidation of this ancient intuition. But no personality test, or series of tests, will ever replace the depth and fullness of the perception of self which can be achieved when the mind alters its state of consciousness sufficiently to perceive the very hologram of itself which it has projected into the universe in its proper context as part of the universal hologram in a totally holistic and intuitional way. This would seem to be one of the real promise of the Gateway Experience from the standpoint of its ability to provide a portal through which, based on months if not years of practice, the individual may pass in his search to find self, personal effectuality, and truth in the larger sense.

## 37. Motivational Aspect.

It is a step by step procedure which involves repetitive practice of the techniques concerned, using each new insight as a means of penetrating farther during the next practice session. But the rate of progress is so much faster with the Gateway approach than it is with transcendental meditation or other forms of mental self-discipline and its horizons seem to be so much wider that the discipline needed to practice it would seem to be within the means of even the impatient, result oriented, skeptical pragmatist of our society. Unlike yoga and other forms of eastern mental discipline, Gateway does not require the infinite patience and total personal subservience to and faith in a system of discipline designed to absorb all the individual's energies over most of a lifetime. Rather, it will begin to produce at least minimal results within a relatively short time such that enough feedback is available to motivate and energize the individual to continue working with it. Indeed, the speed with which an individual may expect to progress seems less a function of the number of hours spent practicing than it is a question of the speed with which he or she is able to use the insights gained to release anxieties and stresses within both the mind and the body. These points of energy blockage seem to provide the principal barriers to achieving the enhanced energy states and focus of mind needed for rapid progression. The more compulsive, the more "uptight" the individual may be at the outset the more barriers he or she will initially encounter to achieving a deep or immediate experience, but as the insights begin to come and the blockages begin to dissolve, the way ahead becomes increasingly clear and the value of Gateway moves from the status of a matter of intellectual assessment to one of personal experience.

## 38. Conclusion.

There is a sound, rational basis in terms of physical science parameters for considering Gateway to be plausible in terms of its essential objectives. Intuitional insights of not only personal but of a practical and professional nature would seem to be within bounds of reasonable expectations. However, a phased approach for entering the Gateway Experience in an accelerated mode would seem to be required if the time needed to reach advanced states of altered consciousness is to be brought within more manageable limits from the standpoint of establishing an organization-wide exploitation of Gateway's potential. The most promising approach suggested in the foregoing study involves the following steps:

A. Begin by using the Gateway Hemi-Sync tapes to achieve enhanced brain focus and to induce hemisphere synchronization.

B. Then add strong REM sleep frequencies to induce left brain quiescence and deep physical relaxation.

C. Provide hypnotic suggestion designed to enable an individual to induce deep autohypnotic state at will.

D. Use autohypnotic suggestion to attain much enhanced focus of concentration and motivation in rapidly progressing through Focus 12 exercises.

E. Then repeat steps A and B following use of the autohypnotic suggestion that an out-of-body movement will occur and be remembered.

F. Repeat step E to achieve facility in gaining out-of-body state under conscious control. Alter hypnotic suggestion to stress ability to consciously control out-of-body movement and maintain it even after REM sleep state ends.

G. Approach Focus 15 and 21 objectives(escape from time-space and interact within new dimensions) from the out-of-body perspective.

H. Use multi-focus approach to solve problem of distortion in terrestrial information gathering trips. This approach involves the use of three individuals in the out-of-body state, one viewing the target object here, in time-space, one viewing it at Focus 15 as it slips into the immediate past, and one viewing it at Focus 21 as it slips from the immediate future. Debrief all three and compare data gathered from the three points of view. If care is taken to insure that the three all go out-of-body together, in the same environment, their consciousness energy systems should resonate in sympathetic oscillation. They can tune in to the same target on different planes(dimensions) with greater effectiveness.

I. Encourage pursuit of full self knowledge by all individuals involved in the foregoing experiments to enhance objectivity in out-of-body observation and thinking, and to remove personal energy blockages likely to retard rapid progress.

J. Be intellectually prepared to react to possible encounters with intelligent, non-corporal energy forms when time-space boundaries are exceeded.

K. Arrange to have groups of people in Focus 12 state unite their altered consciousness to build holographic patterns around sensitive areas to repulse possible unwanted out-of-body presences.

L. Encourage more advanced Gateway participants to build holographic patterns of successful attainment and rapid progress for advanced colleagues to assist them in progressing through the Gateway system.

If these experiments are carried through, it is to be hoped that we will truly find a gateway to Gateway and to the realm of practical application for the whole system of techniques which comprise it.

## BIBLIOGRAPHY

1. Bentov, Itzhak. Stalking the Wild Pendulum. New York, E. P. Dutton, 1977.

2. Ferguson, Marilyn. "Karl Pribram's Changing Reality." Human Behavior, May 1978.

3. Gliedman, John, "Einstein Against the Odds: The Great Quantum Debate." Science Digest, June 1983.

4. Jager, Melissa. Monograph: "The Lamp Turn Laser." Monroe Institute of Applied Sciences, Faber, Va, undated.

5. Monroe, Robert A. Journeys Out of the Body. New York, Doubleday and Company, 1971.

6. Purce, Jill. The Mystic Spiral. New York, Thames and Hudson Inc., 1980.

7. Sannella, Lee., M.D., Kundalini-Psychosis or Transcendence. San Francisco, Henry S. Dakin, 1976.

8. Stone, Pat. "Altered States of Consciousness." The Mother Earth News, March/April 1983.

9. Tart, Charles T. Altered States of Consciousness. New York, Wiley, 1969.

www.ingramcontent.com/pod-product-compliance
Lightning Source LLC
Chambersburg PA
CBHW060043040426
42331CB00032B/2251